The Epistle of Paul to the Colossians

E. Seabrooks

Copyright 2017 by Edward L. Seabrooks.
The book author retains sole copyright to
his contributions to this book.
Published 2017.
Printed in the United States of America.

All rights reserved.

No portion of this book may be reproduced, stored in a retrieval system, or transmitted in any form or by any means – electronic, mechanical, photocopy, recording, scanning, or other – except for brief quotations in critical reviews or articles, without the prior written permission of the author.

ISBN 978-1-946234-07-0

Front cover design by Mark Gauthier.

This book was published by BookCrafters,
Parker, Colorado.
bookcrafterscolorado@gmail.com

This book may be ordered from
www.bookcrafters.net and other online bookstores.

Foreword

Thank you for selecting this volume of the Expository series. These volumes are the contribution of various Apostolic writers. Their biography is on the back cover. The publishers of the Expository series would like to extend a thank you for helping us get this valuable material into the hands of readers.

The desire is that people would read the scriptures and be blessed. These commentary works, or works of Expository subjects, will give insight to, and further the understanding of the readers.

Each of these authors hold the values of the original Apostles of Jesus Christ. These writers want to hold to the values expostulated in the New Testament by Jesus and his disciples. Each of them ascribe to the concept offered by the Apostle John, "I have no greater joy than to hear that my children walk in truth."

Truth has been passed down through generations and has survived critics and doubters. Truth will prevail and ultimately triumph.

These writings are our contribution to the river of written truth that has flowed down through the ages.

Read and be blessed.

Kenneth Bow

Author and Date

Paul is acknowledged as author at the beginning, as was routine in his epistles. Further evidence for Paul's authorship comes from the book's close parallels with Philemon, which is commonly accepted as having been written by Paul. Written in 60-62 A.D., Paul was a prisoner; serving the first of two imprisonments in Rome.

Background and Setting

The church at Colosse appears to have been founded as a result of Paul's outstanding ministry at Ephesus, the effects of which were so influential and far-reaching that "*...all they which dwelt in Asia heard the word of the Lord Jesus, both Jews and Greeks.*" The city itself was declining, but had once been active commercially like her neighbors, Laodicea and Hierapolis. Although Paul may never have visited Colosse personally, he probably maintained contact through Epaphras; one of his converts and associates from Colosse (1:7; 4:12). The apostle penned the letter to counteract the appearance of false teachings that threatened the spiritual future of the church (2:8). Epaphras, a leader in the Colossian church, and perhaps its founder, traveled to visit Paul and report on the situation in Colosse (1:8; 4:12).

Historical and Theological Themes

Colossians contains teaching on several key areas of theology, including the deity of Christ (1:15-20; 2:2-10), reconciliation (1:20-23), redemption)1:13, 14; 2:13, 14; 3:9-11), election (3:12), forgiveness (3:13), and the nature of the church (1:18, 24, 25; 2:19; 3:11, 15). Additionally, Paul addressed the profane teaching that threatened the Colossian church (ch.2).

1.1-8 Paul, an apostle of Jesus Christ by the will of God, and Timotheus our brother, 2 To the saints and faithful brethren in Christ which are at Colosse: Grace be unto you, and peace, from God our Father and the Lord Jesus Christ. 3 We give thanks to God and the Father of our Lord Jesus Christ, praying always for you, 4 Since we heard of your faith in Christ Jesus, and of the love which ye have to all the saints, 5 For the hope which is laid up for you in heaven, whereof ye heard before in the word of the truth of the gospel; 6 Which is come unto you, as it is in all the world; and bringeth forth fruit, as it doth also in you, since the day ye heard of it, and knew the grace of God in truth: 7 As ye also learned of Epaphras our dear fellowservant, who is for you a faithful minister of Christ; 8 Who also declared unto us your love in the Spirit.

1.1-8 Saints. Those who have been separated from sin and set apart to God. **Faithful**. A word used in the NT exclusively for believers. **God our Father and the Lord Jesus Christ**. This designation was often used to underscore the doctrine of the Oneness of the Godhead—showing that Jesus was absolute one in nature with God. Paul illustrates through Greek vernacular (*Kai*) that Jesus Christ is *also, even, and indeed* God--An affirmation of Christ's total embodiment and fulfillment of the Godhead. **Since we heard of your faith in Christ Jesus**. The conviction that God exists and is the creator and ruler of all things. **Gospel** (*euangelion*)—a good message. The Acts 2:38--New Birth message of Repentance, Jesus name baptism, and Holy Ghost infilling evidenced by speaking with tongues is still, and will always be a "good message" an evangelistic proclamation of glad tidings of salvation! The Apostle intended to address the Colossian heresy that had obviously taken up in the church. Unlike the false doctrine or "vain deceit" that was being taught, the Gospel is true indeed, liberating. **Bringeth forth fruit**. Refers to the saving effect of unadulterated preaching and to the growth of the church. **Epaphras**. The likely founder and beloved leader of the Church at Colosse who apparently was saved during a visit to Ephesus.

1.9-14 For this cause we also, since the day we heard it, do not cease to pray for you, and to desire that ye might be filled with the knowledge of his will in all wisdom and spiritual understanding; 10 That ye might walk worthy of the Lord unto all pleasing, being fruitful in every good work, and increasing in the knowledge of God; 11 Strengthened with all might, according to his glorious power, unto all patience and longsuffering with joyfulness; 12 Giving thanks unto

the Father, which hath made us meet to be partakers of the inheritance of the saints in light: 13 Who hath delivered us from the power of darkness, and hath translated us into the kingdom of his dear Son: 14 In whom we have redemption through his blood, even the forgiveness of sins:

1.9-14 The knowledge (*epignosis*) **of his will**—a preposition is added to the word "knowledge," as it intensifies its meaning. This is not an inner impression or feeling, but a deep thorough full discernment of the will of God that is finally and completely revealed in the Word of God. **Wisdom and spiritual understanding**. *Spiritual* modifies both *wisdom* (the ability to accumulate and organize principles from Scripture) and *understanding* (the application of those principles to daily living). **Walk worthy**. Live properly and fully please God. A worthy walk entails: **Fruitful in every good work**, and constantly increasing in the knowledge of God— faith to faith, line upon line, precept upon precept; **Strengthened with all might**, becoming stronger and stronger—desiring strong meat of the Word of God. Patience is preserving through problems, trials and tribulations—enduring difficult circumstances. Longsuffering is forbearing the faults and offenses of others—enduring difficult people. **Redemption**. The Greek word means, "to deliver by payment of a ransom."

1.15-29 Who is the image of the invisible God, the firstborn of every creature: 16 For by him were all things created, that are in heaven, and that are in earth, visible and invisible, whether they be thrones, or dominions, or principalities, or powers: all things were created by him, and for him: 17 And he is before all things, and

by him all things consist. 18 And he is the head of the body, the church: who is the beginning, the firstborn from the dead; that in all things he might have the preeminence. 19 For it pleased the Father that in him should all fulness dwell; 20 And, having made peace through the blood of his cross, by him to reconcile all things unto himself; by him, I say, whether they be things in earth, or things in heaven. 21 And you, that were sometime alienated and enemies in your mind by wicked works, yet now hath he reconciled 22 In the body of his flesh through death, to present you holy and unblameable and unreproveable in his sight: 23 If ye continue in the faith grounded and settled, and be not moved away from the hope of the gospel, which ye have heard, and which was preached to every creature which is under heaven; whereof I Paul am made a minister; 24 Who now rejoice in my sufferings for you, and fill up that which is behind of the afflictions of Christ in my flesh for his body's sake, which is the church: 25 Whereof I am made a minister, according to the dispensation of God which is given to me for you, to fulfil the word of God; 26 Even the mystery which hath been hid from ages and from generations, but now is made manifest to his saints: 27 To whom God would make known what is the riches of the glory of this mystery among the Gentiles; which is Christ in you, the hope of glory: 28 Whom we preach, warning every man, and teaching every man in all wisdom; that we may present every man perfect in Christ Jesus: 29 Whereunto I also labour, striving according to his working, which worketh in me mightily.

1.15-29 The image of the invisible God. In the literal sense, Jesus Christ the profile of the invisible God; in the figurative sense, Jesus Christ the representation of the invisible of God. Jesus Christ is the manifested expression of the omnipresent Spirit of God. Because "no man has seen God" in His invisible state—God made a likeness of Himself in Flesh; man can now see and know him as Jesus. (Hebrews 1:2-3). By describing Jesus in this manner, Paul emphasizes that He is both the representation and manifestation of God. Thus, He is fully God in every way. Both fully man and fully God. (John 8:58; 10:30-33; Heb. 1:8). **The Firstborn** (*prototokos*) or "firstbegotten" or firstborn "among many brethren" — through the redemptive work of the cross. Firstborn also denotes the preeminence, headship, power, and authority—it can also refer to one who was born first chronologically. The supremacy of Christ indicates that he is Lord of all, God of all, and Redeemer of all. **Thrones, or dominions, or principalities, or powers**. A reference made to angelic beings that sit on thrones as rulers, reign over kingdoms, and posses' monarchial and regal power. Paul makes no indication whether these angels are holy or fallen. Though one thing remains the same, Jesus is Lord of both groups. False teachers incorporated in their heretical teaching the worship of angels. The Apostle reaffirms to the church at Colosse that He (Jesus) **is the head...that in all things he might have the preeminence**. Christ possesses immeasurable superiority over any being that false teachers might suggest. **By him all things consist**—that is "to hold together." **Head of the body**. Paul's uses the physical body as a metaphor for the church, of which Christ serves as the head. **In him should all the fullness dwell**. *The Mighty God is Jesus, the Prince of Peace is He; the Everlasting Father, the King eternally; the Wonderful in wisdom, by whom all things were made; the fullness of the Godhead in Jesus is displayed – All in Him ~ George Farrow.* Paul countered the unorthodox teaching that developed within the church in Colosse by asserting that the fullness of deity completely dwelt in Christ alone. **If ye continue in the faith**—to persevere, to stay at or with, to tarry still or still to abide. The expression: **according to the dispensation of God** might be rendered "because of the divine assignment," to preach the gospel to the Gentiles. **Fulfil**—fully preached; nothing withholding. Christ in you. Believers now both the Jew and Gentile, now possess the surpassing riches of the indwelling Christ and the glorious revealed mystery. **The hope of glory** or "certainty of the future."

2.1-23 For I would that ye knew what great conflict I have for you, and for them at Laodicea, and for as many as have not seen my face in the flesh; 2 That their hearts might be comforted, being knit together in love, and unto all riches of the full assurance of understanding, to the acknowledgement of the mystery of God, and of the Father, and of Christ; 3 In whom are hid all the treasures of wisdom and knowledge. 4 And this I say, lest any man should beguile you with enticing words. 5 For though I be absent in the flesh, yet am I with you in the spirit, joying and beholding your order, and the stedfastness of your faith in Christ. 6 As ye have therefore received Christ Jesus the Lord, so walk ye in him: 7 Rooted and built up in him, and stablished in the faith, as ye have been taught, abounding therein with thanksgiving. 8 Beware lest any man spoil you through philosophy and vain deceit, after the tradition of men, after the rudiments of the world, and not after Christ. 9 For in him dwelleth all the fulness of the Godhead bodily. 10 And ye are complete in him, which is the head of all principality and power: 11 In whom also ye are circumcised with the circumcision made without

hands, in putting off the body of the sins of the flesh by the circumcision of Christ: 12 Buried with him in baptism, wherein also ye are risen with him through the faith of the operation of God, who hath raised him from the dead. 13 And you, being dead in your sins and the uncircumcision of your flesh, hath he quickened together with him, having forgiven you all trespasses; 14 Blotting out the handwriting of ordinances that was against us, which was contrary to us, and took it out of the way, nailing it to his cross; 15 And having spoiled principalities and powers, he made a shew of them openly, triumphing over them in it. 16 Let no man therefore judge you in meat, or in drink, or in respect of an holyday, or of the new moon, or of the sabbath days: 17 Which are a shadow of things to come; but the body is of Christ. 18 Let no man beguile you of your reward in a voluntary humility and worshipping of angels, intruding into those things which he hath not seen, vainly puffed up by his fleshly mind, 19 And not holding the Head, from which all the body by joints and bands having nourishment ministered, and knit together, increaseth with the increase of God. 20 Wherefore if ye be dead with Christ from the rudiments of the world, why, as though living in the world, are ye subject to ordinances, 21 (Touch not; taste not; handle not; 22 Which all are to perish with the using;) after the commandments and doctrines of men? 23 Which things have indeed a shew of wisdom in will worship, and humility, and neglecting of the body not in any honour to the satisfying of the flesh.

2.1-23 **Beguile** means to "deceive." Paul did not want the Colossians to be deceived by the persuasive rhetoric of the false teachers. **Spoil** could be rendered, "to be carried away from the truth by false teaching," to cheat you. Here is the term for robbery. False teachers, who are successful in getting people to believe lies, rob them of truth, biblical salvation, and blessing. **Philosophy**—love of wisdom. There are some who will pervert the truth by the supposition of obtaining a "higher knowledge." The uncompromising Apostle calls it as he sees it, **"vain deceit"** or worthless deception. Due to ecumenical exposure, some claim "new revelations" of "how big the Body of Christ really is"—indicating a need (nothing more than a false pretense) to go beyond traditional Apostolic circles; as if there is more! Call it what you will, "higher knowledge" or "deliverance for purist doctrine," at best; all that has been found is worthless deception—Profane and vain babblings, "some professing have erred concerning the faith." **For in him dwelleth the fullness of the Godhead bodily**. (John 1:14-16). Father, Son, and Holy Ghost are not intended to identify three persons of coequal, coexistent, or coeternal status—but three different roles, modalities, and functions by which the one God choose to reveal himself to humanity—with full embodiment in Jesus Christ. Jesus is Jehovah of the Old Testament personified; **and ye are complete in him. Circumcision** denotes a cutting off or removal—a removal of a sinful nature. **Blotting out the handwriting**. The Greek word translated "handwriting" referred to the handwritten certificate of debt, which a debtor acknowledged his indebtedness. We all owe God an unpayable debt for violating His law and are thus under the sentence of death. Through the sacrificial death of Jesus on the cross, our certificate or indebtedness has totally been erased. **Nailing it to his cross**. A metaphor that indicates that forgiveness had taken place. A crucified criminal would have a list of his crimes committed nailed to his cross to declare the violations he was being punished for.

Therefore, the sins of men were "nailed" to Jesus' cross where he paid the penalty. Thank You Jesus! **Let no man beguile you**. Paul warns the Colossians not to allow the false teachers to cheat them of their temporal blessings and ultimately their eternal reward. **Worshipping of angels**—the heresy that would saturate the region around Colosse and ultimately prompt the Apostle Paul to write Epaphras to address this doctrinal deviation.

3.1-25 If ye then be risen with Christ, seek those things which are above, where Christ sitteth on the right hand of God. 2 Set your affection on things above, not on things on the earth. 3 For ye are dead, and your life is hid with Christ in God. 4 When Christ, who is our life, shall appear, then shall ye also appear with him in glory. 5 Mortify therefore your members which are upon the earth; fornication, uncleanness, inordinate affection, evil concupiscence, and covetousness, which is idolatry: 6 For which things' sake the wrath of God cometh on the children of disobedience: 7 In the which ye also walked some time, when ye lived in them. 8 But now ye also put off all these; anger, wrath, malice, blasphemy, filthy communication out of your mouth. 9 Lie not one to another, seeing that ye have put off the old man with his deeds; 10 And have put on the new man, which is renewed in knowledge after the image of him that created him: 11 Where there is neither Greek nor Jew, circumcision nor uncircumcision, Barbarian, Scythian, bond nor free: but Christ is all, and in all. 12 Put on therefore, as the elect of God, holy and beloved, bowels of mercies, kindness, humbleness of mind, meekness, longsuffering; 13 Forbearing one another, and forgiving one another, if any man have a quarrel against any: even as Christ forgave you, so also do ye. 14 And above all these things put on charity, which is the bond of perfectness. 15 And let the peace of God rule in your hearts, to the which also ye are called in one body; and be ye thankful. 16 Let the word of Christ dwell in you richly in all wisdom; teaching and admonishing one another in psalms and hymns and spiritual songs, singing with grace in your hearts to the Lord. 17 And whatsoever ye do in word or deed, do all in the name of the Lord Jesus, giving thanks to God and the Father by him. 18 Wives, submit yourselves unto your own husbands, as it is fit in the Lord. 19 Husbands, love your wives, and be not bitter against them. 20 Children, obey your parents in all things: for this is well pleasing unto the Lord. 21 Fathers, provoke not your children to anger, lest they be discouraged. 22 Servants, obey in all things your masters according to the flesh; not with eyeservice, as menpleasers; but in singleness of heart, fearing God; 23 And whatsoever ye do, do it heartily, as to the Lord, and not unto men; 24 Knowing that of the Lord ye shall receive the reward of the inheritance: for ye serve the Lord Christ. 25 But he that doeth wrong shall receive for the wrong which he hath done: and there is no respect of persons.

3.1-25 **Sitteth on the right hand of God**. Figurative and symbolic in language, not a physical position that Jesus has assumed. "*Thy right hand, O Lord, is become glorious in power;*" thus, an obvious indication of preeminence, omnipotence, and absolute deity of Jesus Christ. **Set your affections on things above**. The Greek word literally says: "Set your mind," "think" or in other words, have this "inner disposition." Let your spiritual compass be set "due north!" In doing so, one must **mortify** or "put to death" the **old man**. "*Therefore* *come out from among them, and be ye separate, said the Lord and touch not the unclean thing; and I will receive you."* The old, unregenerate self, originating in Adam (Rom. 5:12-14; 6:6; Eph.4:22) must be put to death. **With his deeds**. Christ tells us that our ways are not His ways, and our thoughts are not His thoughts; therefore, it is imperative that we rid ourselves and our homes of any "besetting sins" that may be a snare unto us. The new man is the result of a fully surrendered heart. *"I went there to fight, but I'll tell you that night, God got a hold of me."* Just like a baby is born complete but immature, the new man is complete, but has the capacity to grow. **Put on charity, which is the bond of perfectness**. A better rendering is "perfect bond of unity." Supernatural love poured into the hearts of believers is the adhesive of the church. The peace of God is harmony and concord created by God among His people. **Wives submit**. The Greek verb means to "subject oneself," which denotes willingly putting oneself under someone or something. Submission is the true test of self-denial. **Husbands love**. The Greek word for love is *agapao*, the same affection that God has for his children (John 3:16, 1 Cor. 13; 1 John 4:10). **Be not bitter against them**. The form of this Greek verb is better translated "stop being bitter," or "do not have the habit of being bitter." Husbands must not be harsh or angrily resentful towards their wives. **Children obey** (*hypakouo*) — to hear under (as a subordinate), to heed or conform to a command or authority. **Provoke not**. Also translated "do not infuriate," this word has the implication of not rousing up or exasperating.

4.1-18 Masters, give unto your servants that which is just and equal; knowing that ye also have a Master in heaven. 2 Continue in prayer, and watch in the same

with thanksgiving; 3 Withal praying also for us, that God would open unto us a door of utterance, to speak the mystery of Christ, for which I am also in bonds: 4 That I may make it manifest, as I ought to speak. 5 Walk in wisdom toward them that are without, redeeming the time. 6 Let your speech be always with grace, seasoned with salt, that ye may know how ye ought to answer every man. 7 All my state shall Tychicus declare unto you, who is a beloved brother, and a faithful minister and fellowservant in the Lord: 8 Whom I have sent unto you for the same purpose, that he might know your estate, and comfort your hearts; 9 With Onesimus, a faithful and beloved brother, who is one of you. They shall make known unto you all things which are done here. 10 Aristarchus my fellowprisoner saluteth you, and Marcus, sister's son to Barnabas, (touching whom ye received commandments: if he come unto you, receive him;) 11 And Jesus, which is called Justus, who are of the circumcision. These only are my fellowworkers unto the kingdom of God, which have been a comfort unto me. 12 Epaphras, who is one of you, a servant of Christ, saluteth you, always labouring fervently for you in prayers, that ye may stand perfect and complete in all the will of God. 13 For I bear him record, that he hath a great zeal for you, and them that are in Laodicea, and them in Hierapolis. 14 Luke, the beloved physician, and Demas, greet you. 15 Salute the brethren which are in Laodicea, and Nymphas, and the church which is in his house. 16 And when this epistle is read among you, cause that it be read also in the church of the Laodiceans; and that ye likewise read the epistle from Laodicea. 17 And say to Archippus, Take heed to the ministry which thou hast received in the Lord, that thou fulfil it. 18 The

salutation by the hand of me Paul. Remember my bonds. Grace be with you. Amen.

4.1-18 Continue in prayer. The Greek word means "to be courageously persistent" or "to hold fast and not let go" and refers here to persistent prayer (Acts 1:14; Rom. 12:12; Eph. 6:18; 1 Thess. 5:17; Luke 11:5-10; 18:1-8). **Seasoned with salt**—wisdom and grace must be exhibited in our speech. **Tychicus**. The name means "fortuitous" or "fortunate." He was one of the Gentile converts that Paul took to Jerusalem as a representative of the Gentile churches (Acts 20:4). He was a dependable companion of Paul and a capable leader, since he was considered as a replacement for Titus and Timothy on separate occasions (2 Tim. 4:12; Titus 3:12). He had the task of delivering Paul's letters to the Colossians, the Ephesians (Eph. 6:21), and Philemon (vs. 9). **Onesimus**. The runaway slave whose return to his master was the origin for Paul's letter to Philemon. **Aristarchus**. One of Paul's companions who was apprehended by a rioting throng in Ephesus. **Luke**. Paul's personal physician and close friend who traveled frequently with him on his missionary journeys and wrote the Gospel of Luke and the Book of Acts. **Demas**. A man who demonstrated considerable dedication to the Lord's work before the magnetism of the world led him to abandon Paul and the ministry (2 Tim. 4:9, 10). **Archippus**. Most likely the son of Philemon. Paul's message to him to fulfill his ministry is similar to the exhortation to Timothy.

Copyright 2017 by Edward L. Seabrooks.
The book author retains sole copyright to
his contributions to this book.
Published 2017.
Printed in the United States of America.

All rights reserved.

No portion of this book may be reproduced, stored in a retrieval system, or transmitted in any form or by any means – electronic, mechanical, photocopy, recording, scanning, or other – except for brief quotations in critical reviews or articles, without the prior written permission of the author.

ISBN 978-1-946234-05-6

Front cover design by Mark Gauthier.

This book was published by BookCrafters,
Parker, Colorado.
bookcrafterscolorado@gmail.com

This book may be ordered from
www.bookcrafters.net and other online bookstores.

Foreword

Thank you for selecting this volume of the Expository series. These volumes are the contribution of various Apostolic writers. Their biography is on the back cover. The publishers of the Expository series would like to extend a thank you for helping us get this valuable material into the hands of readers.

The desire is that people would read the scriptures and be blessed. These commentary works, or works of Expository subjects, will give insight to, and further the understanding of the readers.

Each of these authors hold the values of the original Apostles of Jesus Christ. These writers want to hold to the values expostulated in the New Testament by Jesus and his disciples. Each of them ascribe to the concept offered by the Apostle John, "I have no greater joy than to hear that my children walk in truth."

Truth has been passed down through generations and has survived critics and doubters. Truth will prevail and ultimately triumph.

These writings are our contribution to the river of written truth that has flowed down through the ages.

Read and be blessed.

Kenneth Bow

Introduction

One of two inspired letters from the Apostle Paul to his younger protégé; the Apostle affectionately calls him "my own son in the faith." Timothy, being interpreted, "one who honors God," received his namesake from his Jewish mother, Eunice; and Grandmother, Lois, who were no doubt believers who began Timothy's early instruction in the scriptures (2 Tim.1:5). Timothy's father was a Greek (Acts 16:1). With origins from Lystra (Acts 16:1-3) Timothy was undoubtedly converted during Paul's ministry in Lystra during his first missionary journey (Acts 14:6-23); and thus, officially accepted the invitation to accompany Paul during his second missionary journey.

A young man, but unmistakably a leader, Timothy received the ordination of the presbytery (I Tim. 4:14; II Tim. 1:6) and was thrust into leadership, often serving as a representative of Paul to: Thessalonica, Corinth, Philippi, Berea, and even serving as pastor of the church of Ephesus (1:3) being at Ephesus when he first received this communication from Paul.

Authorship

Historical biblical accounts support the fact that the apostle Paul was the author of the epistle. The communication itself claims Paul as its writer (1:1), and it is filled with Pauline themes and even contains a brief autobiography (1:11-15). Many modernist critics reject the Pauline authorship of the Pastoral Epistles; thus, preferring to believe that a devoted follower of Paul wrote the Pastoral Epistles in the second century.

Historical and Theological Themes

Written from Macedonia in 62-63 A.D. after his first imprisonment in Rome, Paul writes this first epistle to Timothy addressing certain spiritual discrepancies, false teachings (1:3-7; 4:1-3; 6:3-5); disorder in worship (2:1-15); and qualifications of church leaders (3:1-14). Though abundant in essential leadership directives, this epistle articulates many doctrinal truths as well, such as the proper function of the law (1:5-11), salvation (1:14-16; 2:4-6); the attributes of God (1:17), the fall of man (2:13, 14); the person of Christ (3:16; 6:15, 16); and the second coming of Christ (6;14,15).

I Timothy 1

1.1 Paul, an apostle of Jesus Christ by the commandment of God our Saviour, and Lord Jesus Christ, which is our hope;

1.1 Apostle (*apostolos*) from the verb apostello, "to send one off on a commission with credentials as one's personal representative," of Jesus Christ. The writer designates himself as "Paul." The name is from the Latin Paulus, meaning little. Traditionally, some assumed that his name had been changed from Saul to Paul upon his "Damascus Road" conversion, but this supposition has no concrete basis. His Hebrew name was 'Saul." In the book of Acts, Luke always uses the name "Saul" until Acts 13:9; but after that always "Paul."

1.2 Unto Timothy, my own son in the faith: Grace, mercy, and peace, from God our Father and Jesus Christ our Lord.

1.2 **Timothy, my own son in the faith**. Timothy alone (2 Tim. 1:2; 2:1) and Titus (1:4) received this distinct expression of Paul's approval. The Greek word for son is better translated "child," which highlights Paul's role as spiritual father to Timothy. Timothy was Paul's most beloved apprentice, and protégé (1 Cor. 4:17; Phil. 2:19-22). Further, Paul acknowledges Timothy to be a real believer; in contrast to some whose Christian claims are unauthentic.

1.3-7 As I besought thee to abide still at Ephesus, when I went into Macedonia, that thou mightest charge some that they teach no other doctrine, 4 Neither give heed to fables and endless genealogies, which minister questions, rather than godly edifying which is in faith: so do. 5 Now the end of the commandment is charity out of a pure heart, and of a good conscience, and of faith unfeigned: 6 From which some having swerved have turned aside unto vain jangling; 7 Desiring to be teachers of the law; understanding neither what they say, nor whereof they affirm.

1.3-7 Teaching contrived doctrines of men is a grave mistake. Paul's guidance was based on the fact that others were teaching false doctrine(s); not simply offering a abstract case — and that they (the teachers) would be cursed (Galatians 1:7,8). Timothy was challenged to with preserving soundness in his doctrine, not collaborating with Jewish fables or other non-Christian teachings. **When I went into Macedonia**. Before leaving Ephesus, Paul likely began the conflict with the removal of Hymenaeus and Alexander (v.20), and then delegated to Timothy to stay on and complete what he had begun. **Charge**. This denotes a military order. It stresses that a subordinate must obey an order from a superior. **Teach no other doctrine**. A multifaceted word made up of two Greek words that mean "of a different kind" and "to teach." These were deceitful teachers who were not teaching apostolic doctrine (Acts 2:42; Gal. 1:6-7). **Fables and endless genealogies**. The Jews were known for their mystical dialogues (fables); they added many ideologies and philosophies of commentary to the law. Over one third of Paul's pastoral epistles would be devoted to cautions concerning false doctrines and false teachers. Validation of their Jewish origins was of great significance to the Hebrew people; therefore, pride of race was overarching; pride of tribe was then added to that so that they might not have mingling with neither Gentiles nor Christian Jews. We cannot allow pride to obstruct evangelism. Jesus came to save all men (II Peter 3:9). It is estimated that eight years passed before the gospel left Jerusalem and the Jews, before finally entering into Samaria and ultimately reaching the non-Jewish pagans.

1.8-11 But we know that the law is good, if a man use it lawfully; 9 Knowing this, that the law is not made for a righteous man, but for the lawless and disobedient, for the ungodly and for sinners, for unholy and profane, for murderers of fathers and murderers of mothers, for manslayers,10 For whoremongers, for them that defile themselves with mankind, for menstealers, for liars, for perjured persons, and if there be any other thing that is contrary to sound doctrine; 11 According to the glorious gospel of the blessed God, which was committed to my trust.

1.8-11 **The law is good**. The Greek word for good can be rendered "useful." The Law is useful because it reveals God's holy will and righteous precepts (Ps. 19:7; Rom.7:12). When delivered accurately and appropriately, the law benefits unbelievers in pointing out their iniquities (Rom. 7:7-9) and ultimately leading them to Jesus Christ (Gal. 3:24). The sins Paul mentions are committed by men who consistently live outside the law: **the lawless and disobedient** are those who identify no law over them; they are unruly. The **ungodly and sinner** are irreverent people indigent of the fear of God; thus, showing no reverence for God. The **unholy and profane** are those who "walk on" or disregard holy things; secular, accessible to evil influences. The **murderers** are "smiters," suggesting unnatural treatment of fathers and mothers. The **manslayers** are murderers. The **whoremongers** are fornicators. **Them that defile themselves with mankind** are homosexuals. **Perjured persons** are tellers of untruths; a false swearer. All of these are opposing to the "glorious gospel of the blessed God" or **sound doctrine**—that which is fit and wholesome. Teaching that produces spiritual life and growth, as a result implies that false doctrine produces spiritual sickness and disease.

1.12-17 And I thank Christ Jesus our Lord, who hath enabled me, for that he counted me faithful, putting me into the ministry; 13 Who was before a blasphemer, and a persecutor, and injurious: but I obtained mercy, because I did it ignorantly in unbelief. 14 And the grace of our Lord was exceeding abundant with faith and love which is in Christ Jesus. 15 This is a faithful saying, and worthy of all acceptation, that Christ Jesus came into the world to save sinners; of whom I am chief. 16 Howbeit for this cause I obtained mercy, that in me first Jesus Christ might shew forth all longsuffering, for a pattern to them which should hereafter believe on him to life everlasting. 17 Now unto the King eternal, immortal, invisible, the only wise God, be honour and glory for ever and ever. Amen.

1.12-17 Christ Jesus came into the world — Jesus Christ came into the world to bring salvation from the guilt and power of sin. Christ came to bring men to a life of devotion and holiness and of fellowship with God. Seeing so many who were converted by the supremacy of God, Paul breaks forth with a declaration of praise: "**Now to the King eternal, immortal, invisible, the only wise God, be honor and glory for ever and ever. Amen**." Paul expresses the absolute oneness of God: "the King — the only wise God." God was manifested in flesh. Jesus was not another preexistent entity; He was the one Spirit revealing Himself as the Savior of all men.

1.18-20 This charge I commit unto thee, son Timothy, according to the prophecies which went before on thee, that thou by them mightest war a good warfare; 19 Holding faith, and a good conscience; which some having put away concerning faith have made shipwreck: 20 Of whom is Hymenaeus and Alexander; whom I have delivered unto Satan, that they may learn not to blaspheme.

1.18-20 **Prophecies** (propheteia) or discourse from divine inspiration and emanation; revealing hidden things. Such prophecies, though preceding his ordination, marked Timothy out for his office and authorized the laying on of hands. In times of opposition later in life, Timothy could look back on this appointment and ecclesiastical conferment and remember the confidence in him that was conveyed and take heart. **Holding on to faith**. Paul admonished Timothy instinctively to preserve his own personal assurance and trust in God; while also objectively referring to the body of revealed truth believed by the church, that is, "the faith which was once delivered unto the saints." **Hymenaeus and Alexander**—were men who had deserted "**a good conscience**," and consequently had "**made shipwreck concerning the faith**." We must not be careless with our doctrines and beliefs. As a result, our lifestyle is often determined by our theology and the farther we depart from biblical standards the more susceptible and vulnerable we are to fail in our daily walk. Doctrine and holiness are synonymous. When one is compromised, the other will usually follow suit. As a result of their heretical dogmas, Hymenaeus and Alexander were "delivered unto Satan," or simply excommunicated from the church.

I Timothy 2

2.1-4 I exhort therefore, that, first of all, supplications, prayers, intercessions, and giving of thanks, be made for all men; 2 For kings, and for all that are in authority; that we may lead a quiet and peaceable life in all godliness and honesty. 3 For this is good and acceptable in the sight of God our Saviour; 4 Who will have all men to be saved, and to come unto the knowledge of the truth.

2.1-4 It is practicable that the Ephesian church had stopped praying; accordingly, Paul urged Timothy to make it a priority again in worship—as it should be. Four different types of prayer are mentioned: **supplications**—are prayers that transpire because of a need; **prayers**—a generic word illustrating various kinds of prayer, i.e., confession and adoration; **intercessions**—prayers to God on behalf of others; **giving of thanks**—refer to prayers of praise. There is one explicit reason mentioned for the employment of prayer for public officials: that the citizens of the state, as well as the church, "**may lead a quiet and peaceable life in all godliness and honesty**." Paul's chief reason for the urging is so that the gospel of Christ could be preached and practiced with great freedom. **"This is good and acceptable in the sight of God our Saviour,"** because, as Paul is about to say, God would have all men to be saved (2 Pet. 3:9) and come to **"the knowledge of the truth."**

2.5-8 For there is one God, and one mediator between God and men, the man Christ Jesus; 6 Who gave himself a ransom for all, to be testified in due time. 7 Whereunto I am ordained a preacher, and an apostle, (I speak the truth in Christ, and lie not;) a teacher of the Gentiles in faith and verity. 8 I will therefore that men pray every where, lifting up holy hands, without wrath and doubting.

2.5-8 **There is one God** (Deut. 4:35, 39; 6:4; Is. 43:10; 44:6; 45:5, 6, 21, 22; 46:9; 1 Cor. 8:4, 6) **and mediator**—(mesites) one who intervenes between two; an arbitrator. A mediator "between God and men" must have in his life characteristics that classify him with both God and man. Christ Jesus is such a Mediator. Only Jesus can arbitrate between God and men because he has dual natures. **A ransom**. The effect of Christ's substitutionary death for believers, which He did freely and voluntarily (John 10:17, 18). **Men pray everywhere, lifting up holy hands**—God intended and sanctioned men to be leaders when the church meets for corporate worship. Paul is not highlighting a specific position required for prayer, but merely a prerequisite for effective prayer (Ps. 66:18). The Greek word for holy means "unpolluted" or "unstained by evil." Hands signify the actions of life; therefore, "holy hands" exemplify a holy life. **Without wrath and doubting**—without disputes. "Effectual, fervent" prayer is effective (James 5:16).

2.9-15 In like manner also, that women adorn themselves in modest apparel, with shamefacedness and sobriety; not with broided hair, or gold, or pearls, or costly array; 10 But (which becometh women professing godliness) with good works. 11 Let the woman learn in silence with all subjection. 12 But I suffer not a woman to teach, nor to usurp authority over the man, but to be in silence. 13 For Adam was first formed, then Eve. 14 And Adam was not deceived, but the woman being deceived was in the transgression. 15 Notwithstanding she shall be saved in childbearing, if they continue in faith and charity and holiness with sobriety.

2.9-15 A lifestyle of holiness is commanded for everyone, not just for the women. But it must be recognized that women most often express the peculiarity because of their hair and apparel. **Modest** (*kosmios*) — well arranged, orderly; discreet behavior, not unseemly. Women should neither dress immodestly, so as to exploit their feminine appeal, hindering their brethren from worship; nor are they to incite their Christian sisters to jealously. Women of the world depend on superfluous adornment and artificialities that attract the eye and attention of others, but Paul appeals to a higher principle, that her apparel will be in keeping with her Christian character and role in life — behavior and adornment that befit "women professing godliness." **Let the woman learn in silence** (*hesuchia*) — in quietness; without interruption to argue or dispute **with all subjection** (*hupotage*) — obedience; yielding to a higher authority. Restrictions are set by Paul in regard activity and practice staying consistent to God's hierarchical system and creative design. Neither men nor women should induce one to such a degree that leads one to go beyond those restrictions. Adversely, there must be some condition to the issue of silence, however, it is clear that women are to prophesy and pray in public, as well as teach the younger women (1 Cor. 11:5; Titus 2:4). Nonetheless, Paul appeals to the men directly and the women are to be led by men. Paul was certainly not hesitant to take the controversial stand that authoritative teaching was not the realm of women.

I Timothy 3

3.1-13 This is a true saying, if a man desire the office of a bishop, he desireth a good work. 2 A bishop then must be blameless, the husband of one wife, vigilant, sober, of good behaviour, given to hospitality, apt to teach; 3 Not given to wine, no striker, not greedy of filthy lucre; but patient, not a brawler, not covetous; 4 One that ruleth well his own house, having his children in subjection with all gravity; 5 (For if a man know not how to rule his own house, how shall he take care of the church of God?) 6 Not a novice, lest being lifted up with pride he fall into the condemnation of the devil. 7 Moreover he must have a good report of them which are without; lest he fall into reproach and the snare of the devil. 8 Likewise must the deacons be grave, not doubletongued, not given to much wine, not greedy of filthy lucre; 9 Holding the mystery of the faith in a pure conscience. 10 And let these also first be proved; then let them use the office of a deacon, being found blameless. 11 Even so must their wives be grave, not slanderers, sober, faithful in all things. 12 Let the deacons be the husbands of one wife, ruling their children and their own houses well.13 For they that have used the office of a deacon

well purchase to themselves a good degree, and great boldness in the faith which is in Christ Jesus.

3.1-13 **Bishop** (episkopos) an overseer; one with spiritual authority charged to watch and guard. The terms "bishop," "elder," and "presbyter," are terms that are used interchangeably in scripture, sometimes having a slight difference in the emphasis and connotation. **Blameless**—"not able to be held" in a criminal sense; there is no valid accusation of wrongdoing that can be made against him. Sin, neither flagrant nor overt, cannot and should not stain the lifestyle of a Bishop who must be a pattern for his people to follow (Ps. 101:6; Phil. 3:17; 2 Thess. 3:9; Heb. 13:7; 1 Pet. 5:3). **The husband of one wife**. Greek rendered a "one-woman man." "The husband of one wife" is one who is totally devoted to his wife; maintaining singular devotion, affection, and sexual purity in both mind and action. To encroach upon this is to forfeit blameless and no longer be "above reproach" (Titus 1:6, 7). **Vigilant** means temperate. To be **sober** is to be of sound mind. **Of good behavior** means orderly in life, habits, and work. **Apt to teach**—skillful in the Word. **Not given to wine**—intoxicating beverages are to be prohibited; as should be the case with common believers. **No striker** means not physically violent. **Not greedy** means not fond of dishonest gain. Patient means not quarrelsome, peaceable. **Not covetous**, literally, "not a lover of money." Ruleth well his own house means that he manages his family right. **Not a novice**: he is not a new convert or young Christian. **Deacon** derives from a word group meaning "to serve." Grave means worthy of respect. **Not double-tongued** means saying the same thing to one party as to the other. **Not greedy of filthy lucre** means not greedy for base gain;

hunger for money. **Holding the mystery of the faith** as capable apologists and defenders—preserving the truth as God revealed it. When these qualifications are not applied, we can expect an increase in the number of moral and ethical failures. We need to read over this list occasionally to ensure that we are measuring up to biblical standards.

3.14-16 These things write I unto thee, hoping to come unto thee shortly: 15 But if I tarry long, that thou mayest know how thou oughtest to behave thyself in the house of God, which is the church of the living God, the pillar and ground of the truth. 16 And without controversy great is the mystery of godliness: God was manifest in the flesh, justified in the Spirit, seen of angels, preached unto the Gentiles, believed on in the world, received up into glory.

3.14-16 If Paul should **tarry long** in visiting Timothy, this epistle instructs him how he must **behave** himself **in the house of God**, that is how to properly establish his personal bearing in the church, and how to facilitate church affairs as pastor. **And without controversy**—by common consensus, **great is the mystery of godliness**. **God was manifest in the flesh**; that is, Jesus was God, manifest in the flesh—revealed in human form, but very God Himself (John 1:14; Rom. 1:3; 8:3; 9:5; 1 Pet. 3:18, 1 John 4:2, 3; 2 John 7). **Justified in the Spirit** or vindicated, proved, and endorsed—"this is my beloved Son, hear Him." **Received up back in glory**: Jesus ascended and is exalted "King of kings and Lord of Lords."

I Timothy 4

4.1-5 Now the Spirit speaketh expressly, that in the latter times some shall depart from the faith, giving heed to seducing spirits, and doctrines of devils; 2 Speaking lies in hypocrisy; having their conscience seared with a hot iron; 3 Forbidding to marry, and commanding to abstain from meats, which God hath created to be received with thanksgiving of them which believe and know the truth. 4 For every creature of God is good, and nothing to be refused, if it be received with thanksgiving: 5 For it is sanctified by the word of God and prayer.

4.1-5 Paul had already confirmed the presence of false teachers at Ephesus. He had refuted some of their inaccurate teaching with the positive instruction of chapters 2 and 3. Now he contests the false teachers directly in this passage, focusing on their foundation and content. Paul echoes the warning: "**the Spirit speaketh expressly**," recognizing the explicit warning given by the Holy Spirit to be aware of apostasy. **Seducing Spirits** or wandering and misleading spirits whose purpose is deceptions and doctrines of devils, or teachings inspired by spirits serving the devil. The church cannot wink at false doctrine and trifle with heresy for fear that she be seduced and robbed of her virtue by doctrines of devils. We must be on constant guard and exercise unrelenting observance. When false doctrine rears its ugly head in the body of Christ it must be exposed, confronted, and removed. **Speaking lies in hypocrisy** — hypocritical lie-speakers.

Forbidding to marry, and commanding to abstain from meats. This teaching was probably introduced both by Jewish faction known as the Essenes, and contemporary Greek thought. Neither celibacy nor any form of restricted diet saves or sanctifies.

4.6-11 If thou put the brethren in remembrance of these things, thou shalt be a good minister of Jesus Christ, nourished up in the words of faith and of good doctrine, whereunto thou hast attained. 7 But refuse profane and old wives' fables, and exercise thyself rather unto godliness. 8 For bodily exercise profiteth little: but godliness is profitable unto all things, having promise of the life that now is, and of that which is to come. 9 This is a faithful saying and worthy of all acceptation. 10 For therefore we both labour and suffer reproach, because we trust in the living God, who is the Saviour of all men, specially of those that believe. 11 These things command and teach.

4.6-11 Paul is preparing Timothy in the moralities of being a "good minister." As he does this, he will also be helping himself. Here we have a perfect example of Paul doing what he is asking others to do. He requests that Timothy put others in remembrance of certain aspects of the faith, all the while practicing what he preaches. One should always be willing to do that which he requests of others. **Bodily exercise profiteth little**. The verse may be paraphrased, "for physical exercise is of limited value, but godliness, the result of spiritual exercise, has unlimited value." Reproach (oneidismos)—defamation; the soiling of one's character by strong words and unwarranted accusations. **God, who is the Saviour of all men** in that He has provided salvation for all. **Command and teach**—responsibilities that timid Timothy may have tried to elude due to his youthful age in comparison to those he pastored. A "good minister" will not ignore false doctrine. He will identify it, expose it, rebuke those who are teaching it, and warn the saints of its overt and covert nature. This minister will not and should not be afraid to set the record straight. That is not to be branded as dwelling on the negative. The acceptance of some things naturally implies the rejection of others; the old watchdog remedy of: "preaching against things" still gets the job done.

4.12-16 Let no man despise thy youth; but be thou an example of the believers, in word, in conversation, in charity, in spirit, in faith, in purity. 13 Till I come, give attendance to reading, to exhortation, to doctrine. 14 Neglect not the gift that is in thee, which was given thee by prophecy, with the laying on of the hands of the presbytery. 15 Meditate upon these things; give thyself wholly to them; that thy profiting may appear to all. 16 Take heed unto thyself, and unto the doctrine; continue in them: for in doing this thou shalt both save thyself, and them that hear thee.

4.12-16 **Let no man despise thy youth**. *Despise*—to condemn, disdain, or think little of. **Youth**. The Greek word applied to men 40 years of age or younger. **Be thou** an example: **In word** (conversation), **in conversation** (conduct), **in charity** (love), **in spirit** (proper attitude and volition), **in faith** (trusting God), and **in purity** (without fault in motives as well as morals and ethics). Paul adds: "**give attendance to reading, to exhortation, to doctrine**." Timothy is to keep constant watch over his spiritual life and what he teaches others. He must **continue** in these two activities, for in doing so he will both save himself from the coming apostasy **and them that hear** him.

I Timothy 5

5.1-10 Rebuke not an elder, but intreat him as a father; and the younger men as brethren; 2 The elder women as mothers; the younger as sisters, with all purity. 3 Honour widows that are widows indeed. 4 But if any widow have children or nephews, let them learn first to shew piety at home, and to requite their parents: for that is good and acceptable before God. 5 Now she that is a widow indeed, and desolate, trusteth in God, and continueth in supplications and prayers night and day. 6 But she that liveth in pleasure is dead while she liveth. 7 And these things give in charge, that they may be blameless. 8 But if any provide not for his own, and specially for those of his own house, he hath denied the faith, and is worse than an infidel. 9 Let not a widow be taken into the number under threescore years old, having been the wife of one man. 10 Well reported of for good works; if she have brought up children, if she have lodged strangers, if she have washed the saints' feet, if she have relieved the afflicted, if she have diligently followed every good work.

5.1-10 Paul instructs Timothy in regard his conduct and behavior of the older, aged, members in his congregation. The word elder in both verses refers to those who are advanced in age and/or have been long in the faith. It has no reference to the position of office of a minister. Timothy is to treat elders with dignity, not rebuking or chastising them as he would as disobeying young person, but intreating them to serve as examples for others. To "**show piety**" means to act reverently or dutifully toward. The phrase "**requite their parents**" means to render back recompense. In other words, relatives are to nurture those in old age who nurtured them when they were young.

5.11-16 But the younger widows refuse: for when they have begun to wax wanton against Christ, they will marry; 12 Having damnation, because they have cast off their first faith. 13 And withal they learn to be idle, wandering about from house to house; and not only idle, but tattlers also and busybodies, speaking things which they ought not. 14 I will therefore that the younger women marry, bear children, guide the house, give none occasion to the adversary to speak reproachfully. 15 For some are already turned aside after Satan. 16 If any man or woman that believeth have widows, let them relieve them, and let not the church be charged; that it may relieve them that are widows indeed.

5.11-16 Not all widows are truthfully alone and without means. Financial support from the church is obligatory only for widows who have no resources to provide for their daily necessities. Paul submits three kinds of widows: those "**liveth with pleasure**" (with plenty of resources of their own), those with children or other relatives who may assist with their basic needs, and genuine widows or "**widows indeed**" — who had no visible means of support.

5.17-25 Let the elders that rule well be counted worthy of double honour, especially they who labour in the word and doctrine. 18 For the scripture saith, thou shalt not muzzle the ox that treadeth out the corn. And, The labourer is worthy of his reward. 19 Against an elder receive not an accusation, but before two or three witnesses. 20 Them that sin rebuke before all, that others also may fear. 21 I charge thee before God, and the Lord Jesus Christ, and the elect angels, that thou observe these things without preferring one before another, doing nothing by partiality. 22 Lay hands suddenly on no man, neither be partaker of other men's sins: keep thyself pure. 23 Drink no longer water, but use a little wine for thy stomach's sake and thine often infirmities. 24 Some men's sins are open beforehand, going before to judgment; and some men they follow after. 25 Likewise also the good works of some are manifest beforehand; and they that are otherwise cannot be hid.

5.17-25 **Elders**. This identifies the bishop or overseer, who is also called pastor. **Rule well**. Elders are spiritual leaders in the church. **Double honor**. Elders who serve with commitment, excellence, and effort should have a greater acknowledgement from their congregations. This expression does not mean such mean should receive exactly twice as much remuneration as others, but because they have earned such respect they should be paid more generously. Paul lays out a system of ecclesiastical justice for Timothy to follow. There was to be fairness all around — no partiality, no favoritism, and no cutting slack for close friends or associates, no political juggling of facts or legal technicalities to escape punishment. To help circumvent such actions, no man should be ordained into the ministry unproven: "**Lay**

hands on no man suddenly." As we should know them that labor among us (1Thess. 5:12). **Drink no longer water**. The impure water of that locale may have led Paul to this advice. Further, Paul's seeming approval of Timothy's use of wine for medicinal purpose does not justify its use for other purposes. At any rate, Paul's advice to Timothy simply recommends the use of wine where it may be medicinally helpful.

I Timothy 6

6.1-5 Let as many servants as are under the yoke count their own masters worthy of all honour, that the name of God and his doctrine be not blasphemed. 2 And they that have believing masters, let them not despise them, because they are brethren; but rather do them service, because they are faithful and beloved, partakers of the benefit. These things teach and exhort. 3 If any man teach otherwise, and consent not to wholesome words, even the words of our Lord Jesus Christ, and to the doctrine which is according to godliness; 4 He is proud, knowing nothing, but doting about questions and strifes of words, whereof cometh envy, strife, railings, evil surmisings, 5 Perverse disputings of men of corrupt minds, and destitute of the truth, supposing that gain is godliness: from such withdraw thyself.

6.1-5 The Apostle Paul addresses the fact that it is imperative to accept one's present fate with Christian grace. Believers were to esteem their masters (owners) with obedience and conformity. This kept them from thinking evil of the servant's faith and vise versa.

6.6-10 But godliness with contentment is great gain.

7 For we brought nothing into this world, and it is certain we can carry nothing out. 8 And having food and raiment let us be therewith content. 9 But they that will be rich fall into temptation and a snare, and into many foolish and hurtful lusts, which drown men in destruction and perdition. 10 For the love of money is the root of all evil: which while some coveted after, they have erred from the faith, and pierced themselves through with many sorrows.

6.6-10 **But godliness with contentment is great gain**. Paul is adopting the view and fact that since we brought nothing in this world when we came (Job 1:21), and when we leave it we can carry nothing with us (Ecclesiastes 5:15; Psalm 49:17). That way, nothing the world can give us is any calculation to the person we are. He suggests that we be content with the necessities of life: **food** and **raiment**.

6.11-16 But thou, O man of God, flee these things; and follow after righteousness, godliness, faith, love, patience, meekness. 12 Fight the good fight of faith, lay hold on eternal life, whereunto thou art also called, and hast professed a good profession before many witnesses. 13 I give thee charge in the sight of God, who quickeneth all things, and before Christ Jesus, who before Pontius Pilate witnessed a good confession; 14 That thou keep this commandment without spot, unrebukable, until the appearing of our Lord Jesus Christ: 15 Which in his times he shall shew, who is the blessed and only Potentate, the King of kings, and Lord of lords; 16 Who only hath immortality, dwelling in the light which no man can approach unto; whom no man hath seen, nor can see: to whom be honour and power everlasting. Amen.

6.11-16 The intended communication with clarity, "**flee these things**" — the lust, the temptations, the snares — in so doing avoiding the destruction which will eventually follow. Prosperity is far more hazardous than poverty. No fulfillment or self-actualization lies in riches or wealth. "Let no the rich man glory in his riches" (Jeremiah 9:23). Riches are the beginnings of frustration and disappointment — "Wilt thou set thine eyes upon that which is not? For riches certainly make themselves wings; they fly away as an eagle" (Proverbs 23:5). Contentment is never realized in the sentiment of the rich — the rich man is never fulfilled by his riches.

6.17-21 Charge them that are rich in this world, that they be not highminded, nor trust in uncertain riches, but in the living God, who giveth us richly all things to enjoy; 18 That they do good, that they be rich in good works, ready to distribute, willing to communicate; 19 Laying up in store for themselves a good foundation against the time to come, that they may lay hold on eternal life. 20 O Timothy, keep that which is committed to thy trust, avoiding profane and vain babblings, and oppositions of science falsely so called: 21 Which some professing have erred concerning the faith. Grace be with thee. Amen.

6.17-21 The Apostle is not intimidated by those of wealth or stature — his teaching on this matter certainly doesn't deviate in that regard. He never seems to mind that there are those in his audience — either hearing or reading — who may be wealthy or powerful. **Be rich in good works** by generously sharing of monetary resources with the indigent. He exhorts Timothy not to regard them with more esteem than he should but challenge them not to think of themselves as being above others of lesser means. **That which is committed to**. A knowledge of the truth imparted by Paul. He is to keep or guard it. To ensure this, Timothy must turn away from **vain babblings** (empty or worthless discussion), **and oppositions** (heretical arguments). **Erred**. Going astray from the truth.

www.ingramcontent.com/pod-product-compliance
Lightning Source LLC
Chambersburg PA
CBHW040418100526
44588CB00022B/2871